Over 200
Irish Songs and Dances
That have captured the hearts of music lovers through-out the world

AMSCO PUBLICATIONS
NEW YORK/LONDON/PARIS/SYDNEY/COPENHAGEN/BERLIN/MADRID/TOKYO

COMPILED BY AMY APPLEBY

THIS BOOK IS COPYRIGHT © 2008 BY AMSCO PUBLICATIONS,
A DIVISION OF MUSIC SALES CORPORATION, NEW YORK, NY.

ORDER NO. AM995148
ISBN 978-1-84772-696-4

EXCLUSIVE DISTRIBUTORS:
MUSIC SALES LIMITED
DISTRIBUTION CENTRE, NEWMARKET ROAD,
BURY ST EDMUNDS, SUFFOLK IP33 3YB, UK.
MUSIC SALES CORPORATION
257 PARK AVENUE SOUTH, NEW YORK, NY 10010, USA.
MUSIC SALES PTY LIMITED
20 RESOLUTION DRIVE, CARINGBAH, NSW 2229, AUSTRALIA.

PRINTED IN THE UNITED STATES OF AMERICA BY
VICKS LITHOGRAPH AND PRINTING CORPORATION.

CONTENTS

The Wearin' o' the Green

Traditional

The Harp That Once thro' Tara's Halls

Words by Thomas Moore

Traditional Air: "Gramachree"

1. The harp that once thro'
2. No more to chiefs and

1. Ta - ra's halls The soul of mu - sic shed, Now hangs as mute on Ta - ra's walls As
2. la - dies bright The harp of Ta - ra swells; The chord a - lone that breaks at night, Its

1. if that soul were fled. So sleeps the pride of__ form-er days, So glo - ry's thrill is
2. tale of ru - in tells. Thus Free - dom now so__ sel - dom wakes; The on - ly throb she

1. o'er And hearts, that once beat high for praise, Now feel that pulse no more.
2. gives Is when some heart in dig - nant breaks To show that still she lives!

Erin, Oh Erin

Words by Thomas Moore

Traditional Air: "Thamama Hulla"

The Minstrel Boy

Words by Thomas Moore

Traditional Air: "The Moreen"

Not too slow

VOICE

1. The min-strel boy to the war is gone, In the ranks of death you'll find him; His
2. The min-strel fell! but the foe-man's chain Could not bring his proud soul un - der; The

PIANO

fa - ther's sword he has gird - ed on And his wild harp slung be - hind him. "O
harp he loved ne'er spoke a - gain, For he tore its chords a - sun - der; And

Land of Song!" said the war - rior bard, "Tho' all the world be - trays thee, One
said, "No chains shall sul - ly thee, Thou soul of love and bra - v'ry, Thy

sword at least thy rights shall guard, One faith - ful harp shall praise thee!"
songs were made for the pure and free, They shall ne'er sound in sla - v'ry!"

When Irish Eyes Are Smiling

Words by Chauncey Olcott & George Graff, Jr.

Music by Ernest R. Ball

sweet lilt-ing laugh-ter's like some fair-y song, And your eyes twink-le
spring-time of life is the sweet-est of all, There is ne'er a real

bright as can be;_____ You should laugh all the while and all
care or re-gret;_____ And while spring-time is ours through-out

oth-er times, while, And now smile a smile for me._____
all of youth's hours, Let us smile each chance we get._____

CHORUS

When I-rish eyes are smi-ling,_____ Sure it's like a morn in

Spring.____ In the lilt of I - rish laugh-ter, You can hear the

an - gels sing.____ When I - rish hearts are hap-py,____ All the

world seems bright and gay,____ And when I - rish eyes are smi -

ling, Sure they steal your heart a - way. When way.____

The Kerry Dance

Words by James Lyman Molloy

Based on "The Cuckoo" by Margaret Casson

1. Oh, the days of the Ker - ry danc - ing! Oh, the ring of the pi - per's tune!
2. Was there ev - er a sweet - er Col - leen In the dance than Ei - ly More!

Oh, for one of those hours of glad - ness, Gone, a - las! like our youth, too soon!
Or a proud - er lad than Tha - dy As he bold - ly took the floor!

When the boys be - gan to gath - er In the glen of a sum - mer night,
"Lads and lass - es to your pla - ces, Up the mid - dle an' down a - gain,"

dead, And one by one__ the mer-ry hearts are fled;__ Si - lent now,__ is the

wild and lone - ly glen,__Where the bright glad laugh__will ech - o ne'er a-

rit.

gain, On - ly dream-ing of days gone by, in my heart I hear.

mp

Lov - ing voi - ces of old com - pan - ions, Steal - ing out of the past once more,

And the sound of the dear old mu - sic, Soft and sweet as in days of yore.

Erin! the Tear and the Smile in Thine Eyes

Words by Thomas Moore

Traditional Air: "Aileen Aroon"

Dublin Bay

Words by Annie Barry Crawford

Music by George Barker

Killarney

Words by Edmund O'Rourke

Music by Michael William Balfe

1. By Kil - lar - ney's___ lakes and fells, Em - 'rald isles and___
2. In - nis - fal - len's___ ru - in'd shrine May sug - gest a___
3. No place else can___ charm the eye With such bright and___
4. Mu - sic there for___ Ech - o dwells, Makes each sound a___

1. wind - ing bays, Moun - tain paths, and___ wood - land dells,
2. pass - ing sigh, But man's faith can___ ne'er de - cline
3. va - ried tints; Ev - 'ry rock that___ you pass by,
4. har - mo - ny; Man - y voic'd the___ cho - rus swells,

Come Back to Erin

Words & Music by Claribel
(Charlotte Alington Barnard)

1. Come back to E - rin Ma - vour - neen, Ma - vour - neen; Come back, A - roon, to the
2. O - ver the green sea Ma - vour - neen, Ma - vour - neen, Long shone the white sail that
3. O may the an - gels, O wa - kin' and sleep - in', Watch o'er my bird in the

1. land of my birth: _____ Come with the sham - rocks and Spring - time, Ma - vour - neen,
2. bore thee a - way; _____ Rid - ing the white waves that fair Sum - mer morn - in',
3. land far a - way; _____ And it's my pray'rs will con - sign to their keep - in'

1. And its Kil - lar - ney shall ring with our mirth.
2. Just like a May - flow'r a - float on the bay.
3. Care o' my jew - el by night and by day.

The Dear Little Shamrock

Words by Andrew Cherry

Music by W. Jackson

1 There's a dear lit-tle plant that grows in our Isle, 'Twas Saint Pat-rick him-self sure that
2 That dear lit-tle plant still grows in our land, Fresh and fair as the daugh-ters of
3. That dear lit-tle plant that springs from our soil, When its three lit-tle leaves are ex-

set it; And the sun on his la-bour with plea-sure did smile, And with
E - rin, Whose smiles can be - witch, and whose eyes can com - mand, In each
-tend-ed, De - notes from the stalk we to - geth-er should toil, And our-

dew from his eye oft-en wet it. It shines thro' the bog, thro' the
cli - mate they ev - er ap - pear in: For they shine thro' the bog, thro' the
-selves by our- selves be be - friend-ed. And still thro' the bog, thro' the

The Birth of Saint Patrick

Words & Music by Samuel Lover

Now the first faction fight in owld Ireland, they say,
Was all on account of Saint Patrick's birthday;
Some fought for the eighth, for the ninth more would die,
And who wouldn't see right, sure they blacken'd his eye!
At last, both the factions so positive grew,
That *each* kept a birthday, so Pat then had *two,*
Till Father Mulcahy, who show'd them their sins
Said "No one could have *two* birthdays, but a *twins.*"

Says he, "Boys, don't be fighting for eight or for nine,
Don't be always dividing, sometimes combine;
Combine eight with nine—seventeen is the mark—
So let that be his birthday." "Amen," says the clerk.
"If he wasn't a twins, sure our hist'ry will show
That, at least, he's worth any two Saints that I know!"
Then they all got blind drunk, which completed their bliss,
And we keep up the practice from that day to this.

O'Donnell Aboo

Traditional

Wildly o'er Desmond the war wolf is howling;
    Fearless the eagle sweeps over the plain;
The fox in the streets of the city is prowling—
    All who would scare them are banish'd or slain!
      Grasp every stalwart hand,
      Hackbut and battle brand;
Pay them all back the deep debt so long due;
      Norris and Clifford well
      Can of Tyrconnell tell,
Onward to glory, "O'Donnell Aboo!"

Sacred the cause that Clan-Connaill's defending,
    The altars we kneel at and the homes of our sires;
Ruthless the ruin the foe is extending,
    Midnight is red with the plunderer's fires.
      On with O'Donnell, then,
      Fight the old fight again,
Sons of Tyrconnell all valiant and true,
      Make the false Saxon feel
      Erin's avenging steel!
Strike for your country "O'Donnell Aboo!"

The Daughters of Erin

Words by Thomas Moore

Traditional Air: "Garryowen"

The Cruiskeen Lawn

Traditional

farm - er praise his grounds, Let the sports-man praise his hounds, The
mor - tal and di - vine, Great Bac - chus, god of wine, Cre -
when grim Death ap - pears In a few but plea - sant years, To

shep - herd his sweet scent-ed lawn, But I, more blest than they, Spend each
ate me by a - dop - tion your son; In hope that you'll com-ply, That my
tell me that my glass has run; I'll say, "Be gone, you knave, For Bold

hap - py night and day With my charm - ing lit - tle cruis - keen
glass shall ne'er run dry, Nor my smil - ing lit - tle cruis - keen
Bac - chus gave me leave To take an - o - ther cruis - keen

lawn, lawn, lawn, With my charm-ing lit - tle cruis-keen lawn.
lawn, lawn, lawn, Oh! my charm-ing lit - tle cruis-keen lawn.
lawn, lawn, lawn, To take an-oth-er cruis-keen lawn.

CHORUS.

's Gra-machree ma cruis-keen, Shlan-the gal ma-vour-neen,'s Gra-machree a cool - een

bawn, bawn, bawn, Oh! 's Gra-machree a cool - een bawn!

St. Patrick's Day

Words by Thomas Moore

Tune from Playford's *Dancing Master*

1. Tho' dark are our sor-rows, to - day we'll for-get them, And smile thro' our tears like a
2. Con - tempt on the min - ion who calls you dis-loy - al! Though fierce to your foe, to your
3. He loves the Green Isle, and his love is re-cord-ed In hearts which have suf-fered too

1. sun - beam in show'rs; There nev - er were hearts, if our rul - ers would let them, More
2. friends you are true; And the tri - bute most high to a heart that is loy - al, Is
3. much to for - get; And__ hope shall be crown'd, and at - tach-ment re - ward-ed, And

1. form'd to be grate-ful and blest than ours! But just when the chain Has ceased to pain, And
2. love from a heart that loves lib - erty too. While cow-ards, who blight Your fame, your right, Would
3. E - rin's gay ju - bi - lee shine out yet. The gem may be broke By many a stroke, But

Oh! Steer My Bark to Erin's Isle

Words by S. Nelson

Music by T. Haynes Bayly

1. Oh! I have roam'd in many lands And ma-ny friends I've met; Not one fair scene or
2. If Eng-land were my place of birth, I'd love her tran-quil shore; If bon-nie Scot-land

kind-ly smile Can this fond heart for-get; But I'll con-fess that I'm con-tent, No
were my home Her moun-tains I'd a-dore; Tho' plea-sant days in both I pass I

more I wish to roam. Oh! steer my bark to E-rin's Isle, For E-rin is my
dream of days to come. Oh! steer my bark to E-rin's Isle, For E-rin is my

home. Oh! steer my bark to E-rin's Isle, For E-rin is my home.
home. Oh! steer my bark to E-rin's Isle, For E-rin is my home.

Let Erin Remember the Days of Old

Words by Thomas Moore

Traditional Air: "The Red Fox"

The Bells of St. Mary's

Words by Douglas Furber

Music by A. Emmett Adams

sound of the sea, I know you'll be wait-ing, yes wait-ing for me. The
voi-ces shall sing, For you and me dear-est the wed-ding bells ring.

REFRAIN

Bells of St Ma-ry's, Ah! hear they are call-ing The

young loves— the true loves Who come from the sea, And

so my be-lov-éd, When red leaves are fall-ing, The

cresc. *f*

love-bells shall ring out— ring out For you and me. The

Bells of St Ma-ry's, Ah! hear they are call-ing The

a tempo

young loves— the true loves Who come from the sea, And so, my be-

lov-éd, When red leaves are fall-ing, The love-bells shall ring out—ring out For

1 you and me. **2** *rall.* you and me.

Where the River Shannon Flows

Words & Music by James I. Russell

fair - ies and the blar - ney Will —— nev - er nev - er die. It's the
bless the ship that takes me To my dear old Er - in's shore. There I'll

land of the shil - lal - ah, My heart goes back there dai - ly To the
set - tle down for - ev - er I'll leave the old sod nev - er, And I'll

girl I left be - hind me When we kissed and said good - bye.
whis - per to my sweet-heart, "Come and take my name As - thore."

Chorus.

Where dear old Shannon's flow-ing, Where the threeleaved Shamrock's grows, Where my

heart is I am go-ing, To my lit-tle I-rish rose. And the

moment that I meet her With a hug and kiss I'll greet her, For there's

not a col-leen sweet-er, Where the Riv-er Shan-non flows.

mf

dim.

Down by the River Lee

Words & Music by Adam O'Neill

44

In the Valley Near Slievenamon

Words & Music by Daniel J. Sullivan

Isle o' Dreams

Words by George Graff, Jr.
& Chauncey Olcott

Music by Ernest R. Ball

Dear Harp of My Country

Words by Thomas Moore

Traditional Air: "New Langolee"

1. Dear harp of my Coun-try! in dark-ness I found thee, The
2. Dear harp of my Coun-try! fare - well to thy num-bers, This

cold chain of si - lence had hung o'er thee long, When proud-ly, my own Is - land
sweet wreath of song is the last we shall twine! Go, sleep with the sun-shine of

harp, I un-bound thee, And gave all thy chords to light,
fame on thy slum - bers, 'Till touched by some hand less un-

Danny Boy

Words by Frederick E. Weatherly

Traditional Air: "Londonderry Air"

Oh, Dan-ny Boy the pipes, the pipes are call - ing ___ From glen to glen, and down the moun-tain side, ___ The sum-mer's

Molly Malone

Traditional

fa - ther and moth - er were fish mon - gers too, They

drove wheel - bar - rows thro' streets broad and nar - row, Cry - ing

"Cock-les and mus-sels, a - live all a - live!"

colla voce

rit.

that was the end of sweet Mol - ly Ma-lone, But her

ghost drives a bar-row thro' streets broad and nar-row, Cry - ing

"Cock-les and mus-sels a - live all a-live!" A - live, a-live - o! __ A -

live, a - live - o! __ Cry-ing "Cock-les and mus-sels, a - live all a-live!"

Sweet Rosie O'Grady

Words & Music Maude Nugent

Just down a-round the cor-ner of the street where I re-side, There
I nev-er shall for-get the day she prom-ised to be mine, As

lives the cu-test lit-tle girl that I have ev-er spied; Her
we sat tell-ing love-tales, in the gold-en sum-mer time. 'Twas

Most ev'-ry-one knows,............ And when we are mar - ried, How hap - py we'll be;.................... I love sweet Ro - sie O' Gra - dy, And Ro - sie O' Gra - dy, loves me. me.................

Rory O'More

Words & Music by Samuel Lover

I'll Take You Home Again, Kathleen

Words & Music by Thomas P. Westendorf

I'll take you home a-gain, Kath-leen / A-cross the o-cean wild and wide,___ To
I know you love me Kath-leen dear, / Your heart was ev - er fond and true,___ I
To that dear home be-yond the sea, / My Kath-leen shall a-gain re - turn,___ And

where your heart has ev - er been / Since first you were my bon - ny bride. The
al - ways feel when you are near, / That life holds noth-ing dear but you. The
when thy old friends wel-come thee, / Thy lov - ing heart will cease to yearn. Where

Macushla

Words by Josephine V. Rowe

Music by Dermot MacMurrough

8

72

Has Anybody Here Seen Kelly?

American Version by
William J. McKenna

Words & Music by
C.W. Murphy & Will Letters

Piano.

Mich-ael Kel-ly with his sweet-heart came from Coun-ty Cork, And
Ov-er on fifth Av-en-ue, a band be-gan to play, Ten

bent up-on a hol-i-day, they land-ed in New-York. They
thou-sand men were march-ing for it was Saint Pat-rick's day. The

strolled a-round to see the sights a-las, it's sad to say, Poor
"Wear-ing of the Green" rang out up-on the morn-ing air, 'Twas

Kel-ly lost his lit-tle girl up - on the Great White Way, She
Kel-ly's fav-'rite song, so Ma - ry said, "I'll find him there." She

walked up-town from Her-ald Square to for-ty sec-ond street the
climbed up - on the grand stand in___ hopes her Mike she'd see, Five

traf-fic stopped as, she cried to the cop-per on the beat.
hun-dred Kel-ly's left the ranks in an-swer to her plea.

Chorus.

Has an-y-bod-y here seen Kel-ly?___ K. E.

Mary's a Grand Old Name

Words & Music by George M. Cohan

Peg o' My Heart

Words by Alfred Bryan

Music by Fred Fischer

Oh! my heart's in a whirl, Ov - er
When your hearts full of fears, And your

one lit - tle girl, I love her, I love her, yes, I
eyes full of tears, I'll kiss them, I'll kiss them all a -

heart fond - ly sighs,___ as I sing to her eyes,___ Her eyes of
light of love shine___ from your eyes in - to mine,___ And shine for

blue,_____ Sweet eyes of blue, my dar - ling!
aye,_____ Sweet - heart for aye, my dar - ling!

poco rall.

REFRAIN

Peg O' My Heart,_____ I love you, We'll nev - er part,_____

8va

p-f

___ I love you, dear lit - tle girl,___ Sweet lit - tle girl,___

8va

Kathleen Mavourneen

Words by Annie Barry Crawford

Music by Frederick W. Nicolls Crouch

Little Annie Roonie

Words & Music by Michael Nolan

She's my sweet-heart, I'm her beau.

She's my An-nie, I'm her Joe.

Soon we'll mar-ry, Nev-er to part.

Lit-tle An - nie Roon-ey is my sweet - heart.

Harrigan

Words & Music by George M. Cohan

86

Molly Bawn

Words & Music by Samuel Lover

Mol - ly Bawn, why leave me pin - ing, All lone - ly wait-ing here for you? The

mo - ther, Na - ture, set them sleep - ing, With their ro - sy fac - es wash'd with dew.
knows I'd steal you, Mol-ly dar - ling, And then trans-port - ed I should be. Oh!

stars a-bove are bright-ly shin - ing, Be-cause they've no-thing else to do. Mol - ly

Bawn! Mol-ly Bawn! Now the Bawn!

pp e ritard

MacNamara's Band

Words by John J. Stamford

Music by Shamus O'Connor

* 3rd and 4th Verses sung one after the other without refrain

num - bers we're the fin - est in the land. We play at wakes and
bra - tion, all the gen - try will be there When Gene - ral Grant to
ar - a's band and beat the big bass drum, and when I march a -
look - ing Swede that you have ev - er seen. There's O'Briens and Ryans and

wed - dings and at ev - 'ry fan - cy ball, _____ And
Ire - land came he took me by the hand, _____ Says
long the street the la - dies think I'm grand, _____ They
Sheehans and Meehans they come from I - re - land, _____ But by

when we play to fun - er - als we play the march from Saul.
he, "I nev - er saw the likes of Mc - Nam - ar - a's band."
shout "There's Un - cle Yul - ius play - ing with an I - rish band."
Yimmin - y I'm the on - ly Swede in Mc - Nam - ar - a's band.

92

O Katy O'Neil

Words & Music by Edward Rupert

breez - es that blow All bid me to go where thou art.
you will a - gree For - ev - er with me love to stay.
stay there and tar - ry Un - til time shall car - ry me through.

rall.

Chorus _a tempo_

Sure I al - ways pon - der as lone - ly I wan - der (How my heart grows
(How sad 'tis that
(How fool - ish it

a tempo

rit.   _a tempo_

fon - der a - part.
we are a - part) ____ O Ka - ty O' Neil, how can I con - ceal the
is we're a - part)

rit.

ad lib.

way that I feel in my heart? ____

_mf_ _a tempo_

Savourneen Deelish

Words & Music by George Colman, Jr.

When the word of command put our men into motion,
    Savourneen Deelish, Eileen oge!
I buckled my knapsack to cross the wide ocean,
    Savourneen Deelish, Eileen oge!
Brisk were our troops, all roaring like thunder,
Pleased with the voyage, impatient for plunder;
My bosom with grief was almost torn asunder,
    Savourneen Deelish, Eileen oge!

Long I fought for my country though far from my true love,
    Savourneen Deelish, Eileen oge!
All my pay and my booty I hoarded for you, love,
    Savourneen Deelish, Eileen oge!
Peace was proclaimed; escaped from the slaughter—
Landed at home, my sweet girl I sought her,
But sorrow, alas! to her cold grave had brought her,
    Savourneen Deelish, Eileen oge!

Terence's Farewell

Words by Lady Dufferin

Traditional Air:
"The Pretty Girl Milking Her Cow"

1. So, my Kathleen you're going to lave me All a-
2. Och! them English_de-caivers by na-ture! Tho'

lone by my-self in this place! But I'm sure that you'll nev-er de-caive me; Oh, no! if there's truth in that
may-be you'd think them sin-cere. They'll say you're a charming sweet creature. But don't you be-lave them, my

face! Tho' Eng-land's a beau-ti-ful coun-try, Full of il-i-gant boys—och! what then? You
dear! No, Kath-leen a-grah! don't be mind-in' The flat-ter-in' speech-es they'll make; Just

wouldn't forget your poor Terence, You'll come back to old Ire-land a-gain!
tell them a poor boy in Ireland Is break-in' his heart for your sake!

It's a folly to keep you from goin',
   Though, faith it's a mighty hard ease!
For Kathleen, you know there's no knowin'
   When next I may see your sweet face!
And when you come back to me, Kathleen,
   None the better shall I be off then;
You'll be spakin' sich beautiful English.
   Sure, I won't know my Kathleen agen!

Eh, now! what's the need of this hurry?
   Don't fluster me so in this way!
I've forgot, 'twixt the grief and the flurry,
   Every word I was manin' to say!
Now, just wait a minute, I bid ye!
   Can I talk if ye bother me so?
Och! Kathleen, my blessin' go wid ye,
   Every inch of the way that you go!

Norah, the Pride of Kildare

Words & Music by John Parry

1. As beau-teous as Flo-ra Is charming young No-rah, The joy of my heart and the pride of Kildare: I
2. Where'er I may be, love, I'll ne'er for-get thee, love, The beauties may smile, and try to ensnare: Yet

ne'er will deceive her For sad-ly 'twould grieve her To find that I sigh'd for an-o-ther less fair: Her
no-thing shall ev-er My heart from thine sev-er, Dear No-rah, sweet Norah, the pride of Kildare: Thy

heart with truth teeming, Her eye with smiles beaming What mortal could in-jure a blossom so rare As
heart with truth teeming, Thy eye with smiles beaming

No-rah, dear No-rah, the pride of Kil-dare, Oh, No-rah, dear No-rah, the pride of Kil-dare.

Kate Kearney

Words by Lady Morgan

Traditional Air: "The Beardless Boy"

Mother Machree

Words by Rida Johnson Young

Music by Chauncey Olcott
& Ernest R. Ball

place in my mem - 'ry, my life, that you fill, No
can - dle that's set in a win - dow at night, Your

molto rall.

oth - er can take it, no one ev - er will.
fond love has cheered me, and guid - ed me right.

molto rall.

Tenderly with much expression

Sure, I love the dear sil - ver that shines in your hair, And the

mp espress.

She's the Daughter of Mother Machree

Words by Jeff T. Nenarb

Music by Ernest R. Ball

I was dream-ing last night in the moon's sil-v'ry light, In my
What I saw in my dreams was the truth, so it seems, For I

dreams I was gaz-ing a-cross the blue sea; As she stood on the shore, I could
have here a let-ter that reached me to-day. Sure it's stained with her tears, I've not

Father O'Flynn

Words by Alfred Perceval Graves

Traditional Air: "The Yorkshire Lasses"

PIANO

VOICE

1. Of priests we can of-fer a charm-in' va-ri-e-ty, Far re-nown'd for *larn-in'* and pi-e-ty;

1. Still, I'd ad-vance *ye wid-out* im-pro-pri-e-ty, Fa-ther O'Flynn as the flow'r of them all.

CHORUS

Here's a health to you, Fa-ther O'Flynn, * *Slain-té* and *slain-té* and *slain-té a-gin;*

Pow'r-ful-est preach-er, and ten-der-est teach-er, And kind-li-est creat-ure in *ould* Don-e-gal.

* Pronounced "Slawntia" meaning "your health"

107

Peggy O'Neil

Words & Music by Harry Pease,
Edward G. Nelson & Gilbert Dodge

Nellie Kelly I Love You

Words & Music by George M. Cohan

111

John James O'Reilly

Words & Music by Emma Carus,
J. Walter Leopold & Herman Kahn

that big and strong, He let's noth - ing go wrong, Sure he stops the whole
don't want to boast, We'll live bet - ter than most, And still save ov - er

world with one hand_____ When the girls they go by prom - en -
half of his pay_____ For my man has an eye on the

ad - ing_____ Smile up at him as sweet as can be_____ But he
fu - ture_____ And has hopes we won't have to wait long_____ Till a

pays no at - ten - tion, I just want to men - tion, He's
sweet lit - tle ba - by, Or two of 'em may - be, Can

114

Mickey Donohue

Words by Irving Kaufman,
Jack Kaufman & Frank Williams

Music by Frank Hughes
& George B. McConnell

116

117

The Last Rose of Summer

Words by Thomas Moore

Traditional Air: "The Groves of Blarney"

The Pretty Girl Milking Her Cow

Traditional Air: "Cailin Deas"

1. It was on a fine summer morning, The birds sweetly tuned on each bough, And as I walk'd out for my pleasure, I saw a maid milking her cow; Her voice so enchanting, melodious, Left me quite unable to go, My heart it was loaded with sorrow, For Colleen dhas cruthen na moe.

2. Then to her I made my advances: "Good morrow, most beautiful maid, Your beauty my heart so entrances!" "Pray, sir, do not banter," she said; "I'm not such a rare precious jewel, That I should enamor you so, I am but a poor little milk-girl," Says Colleen dhas cruthen na moe.

3. "The Indies afford no such jewel, So bright and transparently clear; Ah! do not add flame to my fuel! Consent but to love me, my dear." Ah! had I the lamp of Aladdin, Or the wealth of the African shore, I'd rather be poor in a cottage With Colleen dhas cruthen na moe.

*) Irish. Trans:- The pretty girl milking her cow.

Oft in the Stilly Night

Words by Thomas Moore

Traditional Air

The Girl I Left Behind Me

Words & Music by Samuel Lover

The Rose of Tralee

Words by C. Mordaunt Spencer

Music by Charles W. Glover

123

My Beautiful Irish Maid

Words & Music by Chauncey Olcott

125

hearts with joy a - glow._____ You prom - ised, then, you
eyes of I - rish blue!_____ I know you'll keep your

would be mine, In all your charms ar - rayed;_____ I'm here to
prom - ise, love, Tho' stars a - bove may fade!_____ Thro' storm and

claim you for my own, My pret-ty I - rish maid!_____
shine I've come to you, My pret-ty I - rish maid!_____

CHORUS

Oh! my love,_____ how I've wait-ed and long'd_ for

126

Remember Thee

Words by Thomas Moore

Traditional Air

My Wild Irish Rose

Words & Music by Chauncey Olcott

130

'Tis an Irish Girl I Love
(And She's Just Like You)

Words by J. Keirn Brennan & Alfred Dubin

Music by Ernest R. Ball

132

A Place in Thy Memory

Words by Gerald Griffin

Traditional Air: "The Hard-Hearted Maiden"

Love's Young Dream

Words by Thomas Moore

Traditional Air: "The Old Woman"

There Is Not in the Wide World

Traditional Air:
"The Meeting of the Waters"

Words by Thomas Moore

I Love My Love in the Morning

Words by Gerald Griffin

Traditional Air

Oh! Breathe Not His Name

Words by Thomas Moore

Traditional Air: "The Brown Maid"

The Snowy-Breasted Pearl

Words by Stephen Edward de Vere

Traditional Air: "Pearl of the White Breast"

1. Oh! she is not like the rose, That proud in beauty glows, And boasteth that she's so wondrous fair; But she's like the violet blue, Ever modest, ever true, From her leafy bow'r perfuming the still night air. Oh, she's gentle, loving, mild, She's artless as a child, Her clus-t'ring tresses softly flowing down; I'll

2. If I sigh, a sudden fear Comes o'er her, and a tear Stands quiv'ring within her downcast eye; When I smile, those orbs of azure Gleam forth with love and pleasure, Like sudden glory bursting thro' a clouded sky. If I claim her for my bride, She trembles at my side, And gently lifts her eyes with looks so tender; I

1. love thee ev-er-more, Sweet *Col-leen oge as-thore, My true love, my snow-y - breast-ed Pearl._____
2. love thee, on-ly thee, My **Col-leen oge ma-chree, My true love, my snow-y - breast-ed Pearl._____

3. Such was she, but oh! a change, How mourn-ful and how strange, On my lov'd one, my own be-lov'd one came. Pal-er

3. still her pale cheek grew, And her eyes of az-ure hue Seem'd light-ed with a flame, a fa-tal, wast-ing flame. Oh! we

3. laid her in the grave, Where the wil-lows sad-ly wave, And the hol-low winds are sigh-ing a plain-tive wail; I'm a-

3. lone! a-lone! a-lone! So_ wear-i-ly I moan For my lost love, my snow-y - breast-ed Pearl!_____

* Darling young girl (pronounced "O gas-tore")
** Fair girl of my heart.

When He Who Adores Thee

Words by Thomas Moore

Traditional Air

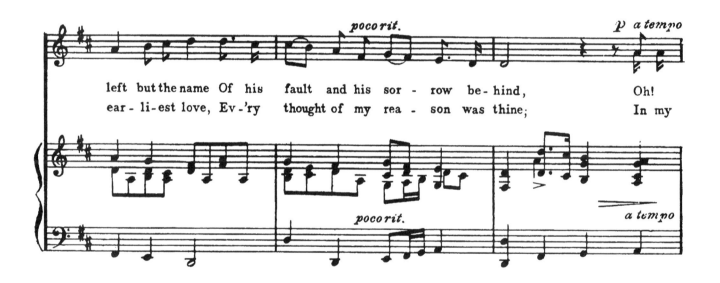

The Low-Backed Car

Words by Samuel Lover

Traditional Air: "The Jolly Ploughboy"

1. When first I saw sweet Peg-gy, 'Twas on a mar-ket day; A low-back'd car she drove, and sat Up-on a truss of hay; But
2. In bat-tle's wild com-mo-tion, The proud and might-y Mars, With hos-tile scythes de-mands his tythes Of death, in war-like cars; But
3. Sweet Peg-gy round her car, sir! Has strings of ducks and geese, But the scores of hearts she slaugh-ters, By far out-num-ber these; While
4. I'd rath-er own that car, sir! With Peg-gy by my side, Than a coach and four, and gold ga-lore And a la-dy for my bride; For the

145

Love Thee, Dearest

Words by Thomas Moore

Traditional Air

1. Love thee, dear - est, love thee!
2. Leave thee, dear - est, leave thee!

Yes— by yon - der star I swear, Which thro' tears, a -
No— that star is not more true; When my vows de -

bove thee, Shines so sad - ly fair. 'Tho'
ceive thee, He will wan - der too, A

too   oft dim   with   tears,   like him,   Like
cloud   of   night may   veil   his   light,   And

rall.

him   my truth will   shine:——— And   love   thee, dear - est,
death   shall dar - ken   mine.——— But   leave   thee, dear - est,

love   thee,   Yes— till death I'm   thine.
leave   thee!   No— till death I'm   thine.

D. S. for Verse 2.

Believe Me If All Those Endearing Young Charms

Words by Thomas Moore

Traditional Air: "My Lodging
Is on the Cold Ground"

-way.___ Thou would still be a-dored, as this mo-ment thou art, Let thy
dear!___ No, the heart that has tru - ly loved nev-er for-gets, But as

love - li - ness fade as it will;__ And a - round the dear ru - in, each
tru - ly loves on to the close;__ As the sun - flow - er turns on her

wish of my heart Would en - twine it - self ver - dant-ly still!___
god when he sets The same look which she turned when he rose.___

f *dim* *pp*

cresc.

The Irish Emigrant

Words by Lady Dufferin

Music by G. Barker

151

Come o'er the Sea

Words by Thomas Moore

Traditional Air

Come o'er the sea, Maid-en! with me, Mine thro' sun - shine, storm, and snows!
Was not the sea Made for the free, Land for courts and chains a - lone?

Sea-sons may roll, But the true soul Burns the same where - e'er it goes; Let
Here we are slaves, But on the waves, Love and li - ber-ty's all our own; No

Too-ra-loo-ra-loo-ral
(That's an Irish Lullaby)

Words & Music by J.R. Shannon

simple lit-tle dit-ty, In her good ould I-rish way, And I'd
hear her voice a-hum-min' To me as in days of yore, When she

give the world if she could sing That song to me this day.
used to rock me fast a-sleep Out-side the cab-in door.

retard

REFRAIN *Smoothly with much expression*
in time

"Too-ra-loo-ra-loo-ral,___ Too-ra-loo-ra-li,

mp in time

A Little Bit of Heaven
(Shure They Call It Ireland)

Words by J. Keirn Brennan

Music by Ernest R. Ball

That Tumble-Down Shack in Athlone

Words by Richard W. Pascoe

Music by Monte Carlo & Alma M. Sanders

REFRAIN

Oh! I want to go back to that tum-ble down shack Where the wild ros-es bloom 'round the door; _____ Just to pil-low my head in that ould trun-dle bed, Just to see my ould moth-er once more. _____ There's a bright gleam-ing light guid-ing me home to-night, Down the long road of white cob-ble stone: _____ Down the road that leads back to that tum-ble down shack, To that tum-ble down shack in Ath-lone. _____

The Band Played On

Words by John F. Palmer

Music by Charles B. Ward

pay day came a - round each week they greased the floor with wax. And
Ca - sey was the fa - vor - ite and he that ran the ball. Of
thank'd them ver - y kind - ly for the fa vors they had shown. Then he'd

danced with noise and vig - or at the ball, ——— Each
kiss - ing and love - mak - ing did his share, ——— At
waltz once with the girl that he loved best. ——— Most

Sat - ur - day you'd see them dressed up in Sun - day clothes, Each
twelve o - clock ex - act - ly they all would fall in line, Then
all the friends are mar - ried that Ca - sey used to know, And

164

on, _____ He'd glide cross the floor with the girl he a - dor'd, and the Band

played on, _____ But his brain was so load-ed it near-ly ex-plod-ed, The

poor girl would shake with a - larm. _____ He'd ne'er leave the girl with the straw-ber-ry

curls, And the Band played on. _____

You Can Tell That I'm Irish

Words & Music by George M. Cohan

Give My Regards to Broadway

Words & Music by George M. Cohan

171

172

CHORUS.

Whis - per of how I'm yearn - - ing, To

min - gle with the old time throng, _____ Give my re -

gards to old Broad - way and say that I'll be

1
there e'er long. _____

2
long. _____

Who Threw the Overalls in Mistress Murphy's Chowder

Words & Music by George L. Geifer

jumped up - on the Pi - an - o and loud - ly he did shout.
we put mu - sic to the words and sung with all our might.

CHORUS.

Who threw the ov - er - alls in Mistress Murphy's chow - der? No bo - dy

spoke so he shout - ed all the louder Its an I - rish trick that's true I can

lick the mick that threw the ov - er - alls in Mistress Murphy's chow - der

The Sidewalks of New York

Words by Charles B. Lawlor

Music by James W. Blake

Because You're Irish

Words by Gustave Kahn

Music by Egbert van Alstyne

1. There's some-thing in an I-rish heart that loves an I-rish song, Of
2. Sure Ire-land's such a ti-ny place to hold so much that's grand, It

I-rish days and I-rish ways they'll sing the whole day long. And
seems to me there ought to be some more of that dear land. And

when you ask me why 'tis you I choose from all the rest, This
in your eyes I see the skies, It's lakes so deep and clear, Sure

lit-tle I-rish song ex-plains just why I love you best.
then it seems I've found a bit of Ire-land o-ver here.

REFRAIN

Sure there's some-thing in the eyes of you, Dear eyes of blue that

shine ___ Some-thing in your voice that thrills me too, When your heart speaks to

Ireland Must Be a Garden
(If You Are a Wild Irish Rose)

Words by George Graff, Jr.

Music by Bert Rule

1. Pad-dy asked a girl from Ire-land how she grew so fair; "Why, Pat," said she, "they grow like me by doz-ens o-ver there. In
2. I'd be-lieve most an-y-thing when your eyes start to smile, It's eas-y to be-lieve nice things a-bout that bless-ed Isle. I

182

Ireland Must Be Heaven
(For My Mother Came from There)

Words & Music by Joseph McCarthy,
Howard Johnson & Fred Fisher

If You're Irish, Come into the Parlor

Words & Music by
Shaun Glenville & Frank Miller

186

The Irish Jubilee

Words by James Thornton

Music by Charles Lawler

sist-ed on the bag-pipes by Fe - lix Mc-Caf-fer - ty, What - ev - er the ex - pen-ses are Re-
then sat down and we looked at the bill of fare, There was pigs - head and gold - fish,
Reed - birds, Read-Books, sea - bass and sea - foam, Fried liv - er Baked liv - er,
Mur-phy took his knife out and tried to cut a pig-eon wing, When the dance was o - ver

mem-ber I'll put up the tin And an - y one who doesn't come be sure and do not let them in.
mock-ing birds and os - tri-ches, Ice - cream and cold - cream, vas - a - line and sandwiches.
Car-ter's lit - tle liv-er pills and ev-'ry one was won-der-ing who was going to pay the bills.
Cas - si - dy then told us to join hands to-geth-er and sing this good old cho-rus.

(After last, Verse)

Should old ac-quain-tance be for-got Wher - ev - er we may be,_____ Think

of the good old times we had at the I - rish Ju - bi - lee._____

The Emerald Isle

Young May Moon

Irish Lilt

The Kerry Girls

The Rakes of Kildare

Round the World for Sport

Royal Irish

Larry O'Gaff

The Humors of Bandon

Strop the Razor

The Tempest

Smash the Windows

The Bunch of Currants

Patrick's Pot

The Growling Old Woman

Top of Cork Road

The Miners of Wicklow

An Irishman's Heart to the Ladies

Jackson's Jig

Paddy Carey

Widow Machree

Kitty of Coleraine

Billy the Barber

Tatther Jack Welsh

Happy Soldier

Full Dress

Old Lougolee

The Connaughtman's Rambles

The Hillside

Catholic Boys

The Praties Are Dug

Swallowtail Jig

Joys of Wedlock

Paddy O'Carroll

Kitty of Oulart

Haste to the Wedding

204

Paddy Whack

Irish Washerwoman

Gary Owen

St. Patrick's Day in the Morning

Champion

The Real Thing

The Beauties of Ireland

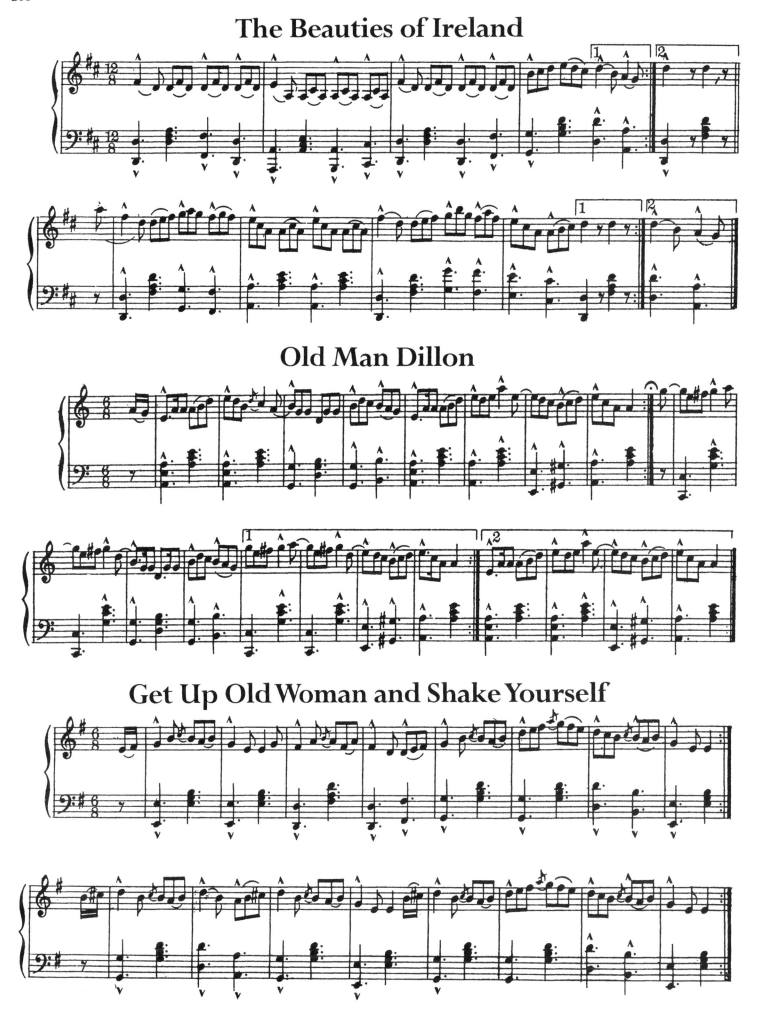

Old Man Dillon

Get Up Old Woman and Shake Yourself

Behind the Bush in the Garden

The Maid on the Green

Shandon Bells

208

Miss Blair's Fancy

The Frost Is All Over

The Clay Pipe

The Joy of My Life

210

The Sprig of Shillelagh

Trip It Upstairs

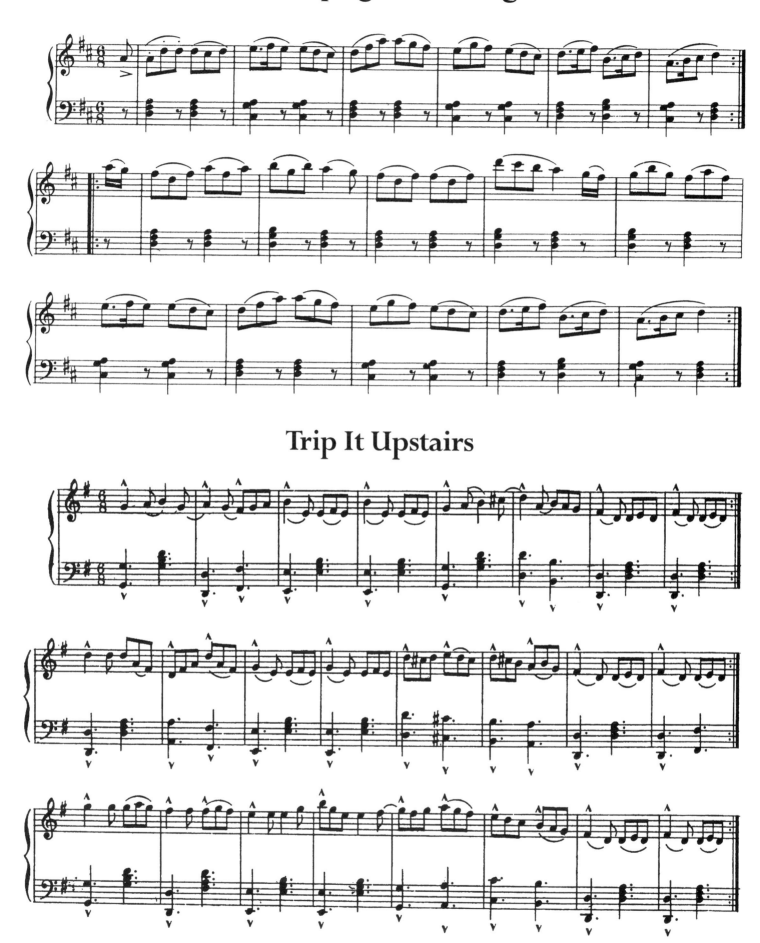

Another Jig Will Do

The Rocky Road to Dublin

Drops of Brandy

Fox Hunters' Jig

Triple Jig

Give Us a Drink of Water

The Rakes of Sollohod

Lep Up

Moll Roe

Silvermore

Barney's Goat

Honeymoon

The Boy for Bewitching Them

Cup of Tea

Emigrant's Reel

All the Ways to Galway

The Bag of Praties

Shule, Shule Agrah

Green Fields of America

The Sixpence

Chorus Reel

The Humors of Castle Comber

Opera Reel

Flannel Jacket

The Devil Among the Tailors

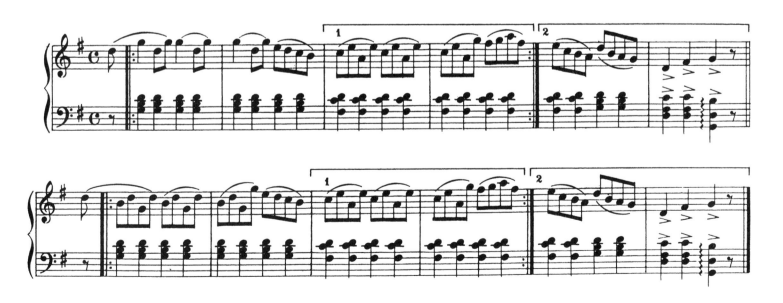

Killdronghalt Fair

Cruiskeen

The Rose

Fairy Reel

The Flower of Donnybrook

Peeler's Jacket

The Wind That Shakes the Barley

Apples in Winter

A Country Dance

Blackberry Blossom

Flogging Reel

Old Crow

Teetotaler's Reel

The Green Fields of Erin

The Galway Reel

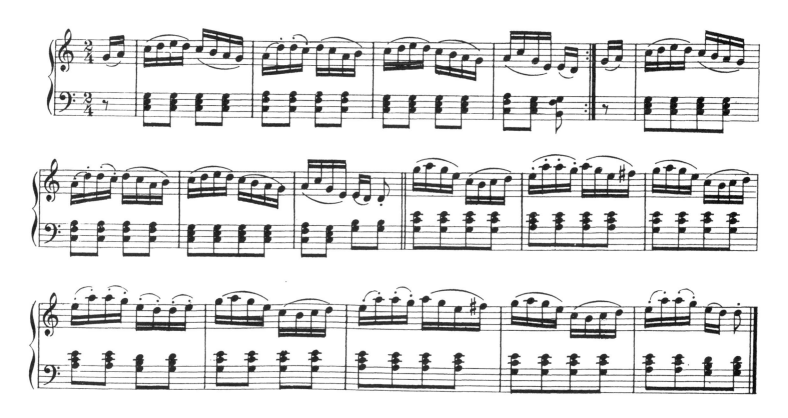

Peter Street

Salamanca Reel

Molly Brallaghan

An Old Reel

Stack of Barley

Guilderoy Reel

Soldiers' Joy

Durang's Hornpipe

Lamplighter

Dick Sand's Hornpipe

232

Hull's Victory

The Rights of Man

The Redhaired Boy

Liverpool Hornpipe

Rickett's Hornpipe

Devil's Dream

The Flowers of Edinburgh

Fisher's Hornpipe

March

The White Cockade

Pretty Lass

236

Patrick Was a Gentleman

Shamrock

Dawning of the Day

The Blackbird

INDEX

Titles in *italics* indicate instrumentals.

The Blackbird

INDEX

Titles in *italics* indicate instrumentals.